Dams and Reservoirs

By Heather Hammonds

Contents

Dams and Reservoirs

Dams are built to hold large amounts of water for people to use. They are built at places where people want to store water, such as at lakes or reservoirs.

a dam made of timber

Water from rivers and streams flows into a reservoir and is held in the reservoir by a dam wall.

Some dam walls are made of timber or earth and rocks. Some dam walls are made of concrete.

a dam made of concrete

Dam walls are very strong and wide.

People can walk along the top of some dam walls and sometimes people can drive cars and trucks along the top of dam walls, too.

Vidraru Dam, Romania

The wall of the Three Gorges Dam in China is very strong and wide.

Three Gorges Dam, China

Dams have spillways. Water flows out of the spillways and goes into rivers and streams at the bottom of the dam walls.

At the Three Gorges Dam, millions of litres of water flow out of the spillway when the reservoir behind it is full.

The water from the Eucumbene Dam, in Australia, is used to make electricity at a power station. Farmers use water from the dam to irrigate their crops.

Eucumbene Dam, Australia

Dam walls hold back huge amounts of water. Reservoirs and lakes behind some dam walls can be seen from space.

Irktusk Dam, Russia, as seen from space

Letter to the Editor

The Global Times

Dear Editor,

I think we need to build a large new dam in the hills behind our town. There are many good reasons why our town needs a new dam.

First, it has not rained much this year and there is a drought in our state.

Second, our town's dam is very small. It cannot store enough water for everyone during a drought. A large new dam would store enough water to last for a few years.

Third, many people are moving to our town, so we will need more water for everyone.

A large new dam would provide our town with more clean water to drink and to use in our homes.

Fourth, farmers in our area need to use a lot of water to grow their crops. They need drinking water for their farm animals, too. A new dam would mean farmers would have plenty of water for their crops and their animals.

Finally, a power station could be built at our new dam. Water from the dam could be used at the power station in machines that would make electricity for our town.

I really hope we get a new dam very soon.

Scott Brady

Letter to the Editor

Dear Editor,

I think we need to build a large new dam in the hills behind our town. There are many good reasons why our town needs a new dam.

First, it has not rained much this year and there is a drought in our state.

Second, our town's dam is very small. It cannot store enough water for everyone during a drought. A large new dam would store enough water to last for a few years.

Third, many people are moving to our town, so we will need more water for everyone. A large new dam would provide our town with more clean water to drink and to use in our homes.

Fourth, farmers in our area need to use a lot of water to grow their crops. They need drinking water for their farm animals, too. A new dam would mean farmers would have plenty of water for their crops and their animals.

Finally, a power station could be built at our new dam. Water from the dam could be used at the power station in machines that would make electricity for our town.

I really hope we get a new dam very soon.

Scott Brady